LINCOLNWOOD PUBLIC LIBRARY
W9-CEC-471

Being Fair

A Book About Fairness

by Mary Small illustrated by Stacey Previn

Thanks to our advisors for their expertise, research, and advice:

Bambi L. Wagner, Director of Education
Institute for Character Development, Des Moines, Iowa
National Faculty Member/ Trainer,
Josephson Institute of Ethics - CHARACTER COUNTS!SM
Los Angeles, California

Susan Kesselring, M.A., Literacy Educator
Rosemount-Apple Valley-Egan (Minnesota) School District

Picture Window Books
Minneapolis, Minnesota

Editorial Director: Carol Jones
Managing Editor: Catherine Neitge
Creative Director: Keith Griffin
Editor: Jacqueline A. Wolfe
Story Consultant: Terry Flaherty
Designer: Joe Anderson
Page Production: Picture Window Books
The illustrations in this book were created with acrylics.

Picture Window Books
5115 Excelsior Boulevard
Suite 232
Minneapolis, MN 55416
877-845-8392
www.picturewindowbooks.com

Printed in the United States of America.

Library of Congress Cataloging-in-Publication Data
Small, Mary.
Being fair / by Mary Small ; illustrated by Stacey Previn.
p. cm. – (Way to be!)
Includes bibliographical references and index.
ISBN 1-4048-1051-X (hardcover)
1. Fairness–Juvenile literature. I. Previn, Stacey. II. Title. III. Series.
BJ1533.F2S62 2006
179'.9–dc22 2005004272

Being Fair does not mean everything is equal, or that everyone is treated the same way. Grownups can do things and go places that kids are not allowed. Older kids are sometimes treated differently than younger kids.

Being fair means that you treat other people the way you want to be treated. This is called the Golden Rule. We can follow the Golden Rule and show fairness even to strangers and people we just met.

There are lots of ways to be fair.

The children all wait in line for their turn to get a drink at the water fountain.

The children are being fair.

Shelly always makes sure to bring enough treats for all the dogs.

She is being fair.

Jean is sure to play the game by the rules even though her dad has never played before.

She is being fair.

So he gets his birthday wish, the kids let John blow out his own candles.

The kids are being fair.

Erin lets an older woman have her seat on the bus so she doesn't have to stand.

She is being fair.

Mike keeps all his belongings on his side of the seat so he doesn't crowd James.

He is being fair.

Jill, Jackie, and Rachel take turns jumping rope.

The girls are being fair.

Jared helps his dad do chores around the house before going to play with his friends.

He is being fair.

Before anyone else gets blamed, Julie admits that she broke the cookie jar.

She is being fair.

The kids make sure everyone gets to join in the fun.

They are being fair.

At the Library

Loewen, Nancy. *No Fair!: Kids Talk About Fairness.* Minneapolis: Picture Window Books, 2003.

Rowe, Don. *The Sandbox.* Minneapolis: Picture Window Books, 2005.

Sykes, Julie. *That's Not Fair, Hare!* Hauppauge, N.Y.: Barron's Educational Series, 2001.

On the Web

FactHound offers a safe, fun way to find Web sites related to this book. All of the sites on FactHound have been researched by our staff.

www.facthound.com

1. Visit the FactHound home page.
2. Enter a search word related to this book, or type in this special code: 140481051X
3. Click the FETCH IT button.

Your trusty FactHound will fetch the best Web sites for you!

Index

Look for all of the books in the Way to Be! series:

Being Fair: A Book About Fairness
Being a Good Citizen: A Book About Citizenship
Being Respectful: A Book About Respectfulness
Being Responsible: A Book About Responsibility
Being Trustworthy: A Book About Trustworthiness
Caring: A Book About Caring